Is Heaven Real?

Meditations on Scriptures
about the Afterlife

ZONDERVAN.com/
AUTHORTRACKER
follow your favorite authors

ZONDERVAN

Is Heaven Real?
Copyright © 2011 by Zondervan

This title is also available as a Zondervan ebook.
Visit www.zondervan.com/ebooks.

Requests for information should be addressed to:
Zondervan, *Grand Rapids, Michigan* 49530

This edition: ISBN 978-0-310-44346-6 (softcover)

Library of Congress Catalog Card Number 2011936909

Compilation and Introduction: Jean E. Syswerda
Cover design: Ron Huizinga
Interior photography: iStockphoto®
Interior design: Beth Shagene

Printed in the United States of America

11 12 13 14 15 16 17 18 /OPM/ 15 14 13 12 11 10 9 8 7 6 5 4 3 2 1

Contents

Introduction

❋

Heaven? Is it a real place? Do those who die truly go there?

To many people — those certain as well as those uncertain of their faith — heaven can seem to be a long way off, to the point where there is nothing real about it.

But be assured, heaven is real! It's promised to those who believe in Jesus Christ! And it's going to be glorious!

The reality of heaven gives
>   Comfort to the dying,
>   Hope to the suffering,
>   And confidence of a life beyond
>   the grave.

God's Word promises a place of
   no suffering,
      no tears,
         no crying,
            no dying.
That's what *won't* be there. God's Word
also tells us what *will* be there:
    Jesus, the light of the world
      and the light of heaven.
      Your loved ones who died
        believing in Jesus.
          Multitudes, singing and
           praising God.
            A blissful eternity.
If you believe in Jesus as your Savior, you
get to go there when you die. All the amazing promises of Scripture about heaven will
be yours. If you're uncertain of your faith,
turn to page 73 in this book to learn how
to be sure and to reserve your spot in that
magnificent place. You can be guaranteed
that your death will not be the end.

Far from it!

Death is only a doorway,
    a split-second leap from this reality
      to the next,
         to a place that's as real
         as the ground
            you're standing on right now.
When you open the pages of this little book, you'll be opening the door to a glimpse of heaven through the eyes of the writers of Scripture and the writers of wise words throughout the centuries.

Enjoy the ride ... from here to eternity.

Surely your goodness and love will follow me
    all the days of my life,
and I will dwell in the house of the Lord
    forever.

PSALM 23:6

Is Heaven Real?

I know that my redeemer lives,
*   and that in the end he will stand*
*   on the earth.*
And after my skin has been destroyed,
*   yet in my flesh I will see God;*
I myself will see him
*   with my own eyes—I, and not*
*   another.*
How my heart yearns within me!

                                        JOB 19:25–27

Speculations? I know nothing
about speculations. I'm resting
on certainties. I know that my
Redeemer lives, and because
He lives, I shall live also.

MICHAEL FARADAY, English physicist,
                                        1791–1867

Is Heaven Real?

We need to stop acting as if Heaven were a myth, an impossible dream, a relentlessly dull meeting, or an unimportant distraction from real life. We need to see Heaven for what it is: the realm we're made for.

RANDY ALCORN

O sweet and blessed country, the home of God's elect!
O sweet and blessed country, that eager hearts expect!
Jesus, in mercy bring us to that dear land of rest,
Who art, with God the Father, and Spirit, ever blessed.

Jerusalem the glorious! Glory of the elect!
O dear and future vision that eager hearts expect!
Even now by faith I see thee, even here thy walls discern;
To thee my thoughts are kindled, and strive, and pant, and yearn.

BERNARD OF MORLAIX, 1146

Stephen, full of the Holy Spirit, looked up to heaven and saw the glory of God, and Jesus standing at the right hand of God. "Look," he said, "I see heaven open and the Son of Man standing at the right hand of God."

ACTS 7:55–56

We can proceed with bold assurance, thanks to the evidence of history that established with convincing clarity how Jesus not only preceded us in death but also came back from the dead and blazed the trail to heaven.

LEE STROBEL

I once scorned ev'ry fearful thought of death,
When it was but the end of pulse and breath,
But now my eyes have seen that past the pain
There is a world that's waiting to be claimed.

Earthmaker, Holy, let me now depart,
For living's such a temporary art.
And dying is but getting dressed for God,
Our graves are merely doorways cut in sod.

CALVIN MILLER

But our citizenship is in heaven. And we eagerly await a Savior from there, the Lord Jesus Christ, who, by the power that enables him to bring everything under his control, will transform our lowly bodies so that they will be like his glorious body.

PHILIPPIANS 3:20–21

The big, blazing, terrible truth about man is that he has a heaven-sized hole in his heart, and nothing else can fill it.

PETER KREEFT

* * *

After this I looked, and there before me was a great multitude that no one could count, from every nation, tribe, people and language, standing before the throne and before the Lamb. They were wearing white robes and were holding palm branches in their hands. And they cried out in a loud voice:

> *"Salvation belongs to our God,*
> *who sits on the throne,*
> *and to the Lamb."*

REVELATION 7:9–10

* * *

The book of Revelation describes a scene from the future in which Jesus himself embraces and restores all those who have suffered and died ... That scene reminds me that heaven is our true destiny, however good life on earth seems to be. Heaven is our real home, where we have always longed to be.

JERRY SITTSER

There's nothing outside heaven except hell. Earth is not outside heaven; it is heaven's workshop, heaven's womb.

PETER KREEFT

In the hope of eternal life, which God, who does not lie, promised before the beginning of time.

TITUS 1:2

Something deep within us tells us that death is not natural. We fight against it as if it is a foreign enemy, and in a sense it is. God has placed eternity into the heart of every person, so we long for life to go on, yet we are so attached to life on earth that we resist heaven, the true home Jesus has prepared for us.

DAVE DRAVECKY

Finish, then, Thy new creation;
Pure and spotless let us be.
Let us see Thy great salvation
Perfectly restored in Thee;
Changed from glory into glory,
Till in heaven we take our place,
Till we cast our crowns before Thee,
Lost in wonder, love, and praise.

CHARLES WESLEY, 1747

*Elijah went up to heaven
in a whirlwind.*

2 KINGS 2:11

As any good child in Sunday school, I believed that heaven was "up" ... distances like "up" and "down" lose their meaning when you realize that heaven — even the highest heavens — exist beyond our space-time continuum ... Step beyond the edge of outer space and you enter the fifth dimension where gargantuan distances light-years long are a snap of the finger to, well ... to the dying thief who, when he died, instantly appeared in paradise alongside Jesus.

JONI EARECKSON TADA

After the Lord Jesus had spoken to them, he was taken up into heaven and he sat at the right hand of God.

MARK 16:19

Jesus [made] this astonishing claim: "There *is* life after death. It's not fantasy, it's not make-believe, and it's not wishful thinking. In fact, I'll prove it to you by bringing Lazarus back to life after his four days in a tomb. And later I'll establish it conclusively by overcoming the grave myself."

LEE STROBEL

"Do not let your hearts be troubled. You believe in God; believe also in me. My Father's house has many rooms; if that were not so, would I have told you that I am going there to prepare a place for you? And if I go and prepare a place for you, I will come back and take you to be with me that you also may be where I am."

JOHN 14:1–3

What know we of the country to which we are bound? A little we have read thereof, and somewhat has been revealed to us by the Spirit; but how little do we know of the realms of the future! ... What wonder-world will open upon our astonished sight? What scene of glory will be unfolded to our view? No traveller has ever returned to tell. But we know enough of the heavenly land to make us welcome our summons thither with joy and gladness ... We shall be departing from all we have known and loved here, but we shall be going to our Father's house—to our Father's home, where Jesus is—to that royal "city which hath foundations, whose builder and maker is God." This shall be our last removal, to dwell forever with him we love, in the midst of his people, in the presence of God.

CHARLES SPURGEON, 1834–1892

21

There's a land that is fairer than day,
And by faith we can see it afar;
For the Father waits over the way
To prepare us a dwelling place there.

In the sweet by and by,
We shall meet on that beautiful shore;
In the sweet by and by,
We shall meet on that beautiful shore.

SANFORD F. BENNETT, 1868

[Jacob] had a dream in which he saw a stairway resting on the earth, with its top reaching to heaven, and the angels of God were ascending and descending on it. There above it stood the LORD ... When Jacob awoke from his sleep, he thought, "Surely the LORD is in this place ... This is none other than the house of God; this is the gate of heaven."

GENESIS 28:12–13,16–17

Something inside me knew that God had healed Maria in a way we didn't want ... Somehow in that unthinkable moment it became clear to Steven and me that we were standing at the very door of heaven, placing our little girl carefully in the arms of Jesus, desperately trusting that she would be safe there until we could come and join her.

MARY BETH CHAPMAN

I tell you a mystery: We will not all sleep, but we will all be changed—in a flash, in the twinkling of an eye, at the last trumpet. For the trumpet will sound, the dead will be raised imperishable, and we will be changed. For the perishable must clothe itself with the imperishable, and the mortal with immortality. When the perishable has been clothed with the imperishable, and the mortal with immortality, then the saying that is written will come true: "Death has been swallowed up in victory."

"Where, O death, is your victory?
Where, O death, is your sting?"

The sting of death is sin, and the power of sin is the law. But thanks be to God! He gives us the victory through our Lord Jesus Christ.

1 CORINTHIANS 15:51–57

Is Heaven Real?

Earth recedes, heaven opens.
I've been through the gates!
Don't call me back ...
if this is death, it's sweet.

DWIGHT L. MOODY, 1837–1899

*Therefore my heart is glad and my tongue
rejoices;*
my body also will rest secure,
*because you will not abandon me to the
realm of the dead ...*
*you will fill me with joy in your presence,
with eternal pleasures at your right hand.*

PSALM 16:9–11

Some day you will read in the papers that D.L. Moody is dead. Don't you believe a word of it! At that moment I shall be more alive than I am now; I shall have gone up higher, that is all, out of this old clay tenement into a house that is immortal—a body that death cannot touch, that sin cannot taint; a body fashioned like unto His glorious body.

DWIGHT L. MOODY, 1837-1899

But sin and flesh, dust and pain, will all be left behind together. O the blessed tranquility of that region, where there is nothing but sweet continued peace! O healthful place, where none are sick! O fortunate land, where all are kings! O holy assembly, where all are priests! How free a state, where none are servants but to their supreme Monarch! The poor man shall no more be tired with his labors: no more hunger or thirst, cold or nakedness: no pinching frosts or scorching heats. Our faces shall no more be pale or sad; no more breaches in friendship, nor parting of friends asunder; no more trouble accompanying our relations, nor voice of lamentation heard in our dwellings: God shall wipe away all tears from our eyes. O my soul, bear with the infirmities of thine earthly tabernacle; it will be thus but a little while; the sound of thy Redeemer's feet is even at the door.

RICHARD BAXTER, 1615–1691

So will it be with the resurrection of the dead. The body that is sown is perishable, it is raised imperishable; it is sown in dishonor, it is raised in glory; it is sown in weakness, it is raised in power; it is sown a natural body, it is raised a spiritual body.

1 CORINTHIANS 15:42–44

For we know that if the earthly tent we live in is destroyed, we have a building from God, an eternal house in heaven, not built by human hands.

2 CORINTHIANS 5:1

If I find in myself a desire
which no experience in this world can satisfy,
the most probable explanation
is that I was made for another world.

C. S. LEWIS

Praise be to the God and Father of our Lord Jesus Christ! In his great mercy he has given us new birth into a living hope through the resurrection of Jesus Christ from the dead, and into an inheritance that can never perish, spoil or fade. This inheritance is kept in heaven for you.

1 PETER 1:3–4

[Death] is not the end. I thank God that I know that this is not all there is. My whole everlasting being, my entire personality — all that I have and all that I am are cast out on the promises of God that there is another chapter! At the close of every obituary of his believing children, God adds the word *henceforth!* After every biography, God adds the word *henceforth!* There will be a tomorrow and this is the reason for Christian joy.

A. W. TOZER

You have come to Mount Zion, to the city of the living God, the heavenly Jerusalem. You have come to thousands upon thousands of angels in joyful assembly ... You have come to God, the Judge of all ... to Jesus the mediator of a new covenant.

HEBREWS 12:22–24

All your life an unattainable ecstasy has hovered just beyond the grasp of your consciousness. The day is coming when you will wake to find, beyond all hope, that you have attained it.

C. S. LEWIS

God will redeem me from the realm of the dead;
he will surely take me to himself.

PSALM 49:15

I shall not live till I see God;
and when I have seen Him,
I shall never die.

JOHN DONNE

✻

Rejoice in that day and leap for joy, because great is your reward in heaven.

LUKE 6:23

✻

*"… no eye has seen,
… no ear has heard,
… no human mind has conceived"—
the things God has prepared
for those who love him.*

1 CORINTHIANS 2:9

✻

What Is Heaven Like?

Then I saw ... heaven ... I heard a loud voice from the throne saying, "Look! God's dwelling place is now among the people, and he will dwell with them. They will be his people, and God himself will be with them and be their God. 'He will wipe every tear from their eyes. There will be no more death' or mourning or crying or pain."

REVELATION 21:1,3–4

Someday God will wipe away your tears. The same hands that stretched the heavens will touch your cheeks. The same hands that formed the mountains will caress your face. The same hands that curled in agony as the Roman spike cut through will someday cup your face and brush away your tears. Forever. When you think of a world where there will be no reason to cry, ever, doesn't it make you want to go home?

MAX LUCADO

O then, what a blessed day will that be when I shall ... stand on the shore and look back on the raging seas I have safely passed; when I shall review my pains and sorrows, my fears and tears, and possess the glory which was the end of all!

RICHARD BAXTER, 1615–1691

To come to thee is to come home from exile, to come to land out of the raging storm, to come to rest after long labour, to come to the goal of my desires and the summit of my wishes.

CHARLES SPURGEON, 1834–1892

"Dad, nobody's old in heaven," Colton said. "And nobody wears glasses."

TODD BURPO

"And God will wipe away every tear from their eyes."

REVELATION 7:17

Is Heaven Real?

There is no grief in Heaven;
For life is one glad day;
And tears are of those former things
Which all have passed away.

There is no sin in Heaven;
Behold that blessed throng:
All holy is their spotless robe,
All holy is their song!

There is no death in Heaven;
For they who gain that shore
Have won their immortality,
And they can die no more.

FRANCIS M. KNOLLIS, 1859

The joys of heaven will surely compensate for the sorrows of earth. Hush, hush, my doubts! death is but a narrow stream, and thou shalt soon have forded it. Time, how short — eternity, how long! Death, how brief — immortality, how endless!

CHARLES SPURGEON, 1834 – 1892

They will see his face.

REVELATION 22:4

Some day the silver cord will break,
And I no more as now shall sing;
But oh, the joy when I shall wake
Within the palace of the King!

And I shall see Him face to face,
And tell the story — Saved by grace;
And I shall see Him face to face,
And tell the story — Saved by grace.

Some day my earthly house will fall.
I cannot tell how soon 'twill be;
But this I know — my All in All
Has now a place in Heav'n for me.

FANNY CROSBY, 1891

Death ... is no more than passing from one room into another. But there's a difference for me, you know. Because in that other room I shall be able to see.

HELEN KELLER

Whom have I in heaven but you?
And earth has nothing I desire besides you.

PSALM 73:25

To go to heaven, fully to enjoy God, is infinitely better than the most pleasant accommodations here. Fathers and mothers, husbands, wives, or children, or the company of earthly friends, are but shadows; but God is the substance. These are but scattered beams, but God is the sun. These are but streams. But God is the ocean.

JONATHAN EDWARDS, 1703–1758

I like earth. But my heart pumps for heaven. Our hearts hold a shadow of heaven … I have a glorious homesickness for heaven, a penetrating and piercing ache. I'm a stranger in a strange land, a displaced person … What a sweetness to feel homesick for heaven.

JONI EARECKSON TADA

But our citizenship is in heaven. And we eagerly await a Savior from there, the Lord Jesus Christ, who, by the power that enables him to bring everything under his control, will transform our lowly bodies so that they will be like his glorious body.

PHILIPPIANS 3:20–21

I now know the meaning of being "glorified."
It's the time, after my death here,
when I'll be on my feet dancing.

JONI EARECKSON TADA

What will it be like for those who died weak and elderly to take their first steps in their resurrected bodies? In C. S. Lewis's *The Last Battle*, on entering heaven Lord Digory says he and Lady Polly have been "unstiffened" … I look forward to seeing my mother and father "unstiffened" again — and to being completely unstiffened myself!

RANDY ALCORN

One day [we] will have a new body, light, bright, and clothed in righteousness — powerful and dazzling. No other religion, no other philosophy promises new bodies, hearts and minds. Only in the Gospel of Christ do hurting people find such incredible hope.

JONI EARECKSON TADA

I saw the Holy City, the new Jerusalem, coming down out of heaven from God, prepared as a bride beautifully dressed for her husband.

REVELATION 21:2

What Is Heaven Like?

[The new Jerusalem:] Everything is gone that ever made Jerusalem, like all cities, torn apart, dangerous, heartbreaking, seamy ... The city has become what those who loved it always dreamed and what in their dreams she always was. The new Jerusalem. That seems to be the secret of heaven. The new Chicago, Leningrad, Hiroshima, Beirut. The new bus driver, hot-dog man, seamstress, hairdresser. The new you, me, everybody.

FREDERICK BUECHNER

O what is He providing for me? What entertainment with Him shall I shortly find? Not such as He found with man, when He came to seek us. It is not a manger, a crown of thorns, a cross, that He is preparing for me. When I have had my part of these in following Him, I shall have my place in the glorious Jerusalem.

MARGARET CHARLTON BAXTER, 1631–1681

Is Heaven Real?

*I heard a sound from heaven like the roar
of rushing waters and like a loud peal of
thunder. The sound I heard was like that
of harpists playing their harps. And they
sang a new song before the throne.*

REVELATION 14:2–3

Even today, the single, most vivid memory I have
of my entire heavenly experience [was] music,
but it differed from anything I had ever heard
or ever expect to hear on earth. The melodies
of praise filled the atmosphere. The non-stop
intensity and endless variety overwhelmed me.

DON PIPER

Let's not get too settled in, too satisfied
with the good things down here on earth.
They are only the tinkling sounds of the
orchestra warming up. The real song is
about to break into a heavenly symphony,
and its prelude is only a few moments away.

JONI EARECKSON TADA

What Is Heaven Like?

There's no disappointment in Heaven,
No weariness, sorrow or pain;
No hearts that are bleeding and broken,
No song with a minor refrain.
The clouds of our earthly horizon
Will never appear in the sky,
For all will be sunshine and gladness,
With never a sob or a sigh.

I'm bound for that beautiful city,
My Lord has prepared for His own;
Where all the redeemed of all ages
Sing "Glory!" around the white throne;
Sometimes I grow homesick for Heaven,
And the glories I there shall behold;
What a joy that will be when my Savior I see,
In that beautiful city of gold.

FREDERICK M. LEHMAN, 1914

*Then I heard a voice from heaven say,
"Write this: Blessed are the dead
who die in the Lord from now on."
"Yes," says the Spirit, "they will rest
from their labor, for their deeds
will follow them."*

REVELATION 14:13

Desire is a signpost pointing to Heaven. Every longing for better health is a longing for the New Earth. Every longing for romance is a longing for the ultimate romance with Christ. Every desire for intimacy is a desire for Christ. Every thirst for beauty is a thirst for Christ. Every taste of joy is but a foretaste of a greater and more vibrant joy than can be found on Earth as it is now.

RANDY ALCORN

Earth is a "sometimes joy" experience. As deeply as we might know Christ, and as much as we might have faith in Him, our joy here is not constant because we live in a world of circumstances that frequently rob us of joy. Heaven, on the other hand, is an "always joy" experience. It is a place of supreme happiness.

ZIG ZIGLAR

The world separates humor and seriousness; heaven joins them. The world can't be serious and joyful at the same time; if this is all there is, it's pretty grim, and joy is mere comic relief. But heavenly joy is not comic relief ... It is not an outlet of tension, a vacation from dull, onerous everydayness. It is the everyday work of heaven; heaven's work is play!

PETER KREEFT

Is Heaven Real?

My cup doth often while below,
With Marah's waters overflow:
But care and grief which here annoy,
Above shall be absorbed in joy.
Crumbs are on earth our richest fare:
But banquets wait the pilgrim there.
Here cold and faint the songs we raise:
But deathless there will be our praise.
Here evening shades envelope me;
All darkness shall from Zion flee;
Without a veil it will be given
God face to face to see in Heaven.

WELSH HYMN

After this I heard what sounded like
the roar of a great multitude in heaven
shouting: "Hallelujah! Salvation and
glory and power belong to our God."

REVELATION 19:1

The shepherds of the Alps have a beautiful custom of ending the day by singing an evening farewell to one another. The air is so pure that the songs can be heard for very long distances. As the sun begins to set, they gather their flocks and begin to lead them down the mountain paths while they sing, "'Thus far has the Lord helped us,' Let us praise His name!"

Finally ... they sing to one another the courteous and friendly farewell "Goodnight! Goodnight!" The words then begin to echo from mountainside to mountainside, reverberating sweetly and softly until the music fades into the distance.

Let us also call out to one another through the darkness until the night becomes alive with the sound of many voices, encouraging God's weary travelers. And may echoes grow into a storm of hallelujahs that will break in thundering waves around His sapphire throne. Then as the morning dawns, we will find ourselves on the shore of the "sea of glass," crying out with the redeemed hosts of heaven, "To him who sits on the throne and to the Lamb be praise and honor and glory and power, for ever and ever!" (Rev. 5:13)

L. B. COWMAN

Yes, we will have a new song. It is the song of Moses and the Lamb. I don't know just who wrote it or how, but it will be a glorious song. I suppose the singing we have here on earth will be nothing compared with the songs of the upper world ... It seems to me if we are truly children of God, we will want to sing about it. And so, when we get there, we can't help shouting out the loud hallelujahs of heaven.

DWIGHT L. MOODY, 1837–1899

Praise will not be something we will be assigned or commanded to do; it will be natural. In heaven, we, like diamonds, will give off prism-like praise as every facet of our being reflects His Shekinah glory ... A supernatural effervescent response of the born-again creature, new and fit for heaven. It will be impossible not to praise Him.

JONI EARECKSON TADA

If you are not allowed
to laugh in heaven,
I don't want to go there.

MARTIN LUTHER

There will be no more night. They will not need the light of a lamp or the light of the sun, for the Lord God will give them light. And they will reign for ever and ever.

REVELATION 22:5

Heaven's light and texture defy earthly eyes or explanation. Warm, radiant light engulfed me. As I looked around, I could hardly grasp the vivid, dazzling colors. Every hue and tone surpassed anything I had ever seen.

DON PIPER

The city does not need the sun or the moon to shine on it, for the glory of God gives it light, and the Lamb is its lamp. The nations will walk by its light, and the kings of the earth will bring their splendor into it. On no day will its gates ever be shut, for there will be no night there. The glory and honor of the nations will be brought into it. Nothing impure will ever enter it, nor will anyone who does what is shameful or deceitful, but only those whose names are written in the Lamb's book of life.

REVELATION 21:23–27

What Is Heaven Like?

We are heading for a *new* reality ... not a fundamentally *different* reality. We are not leaving the created order for some other "spiritual" order. Rather, we will be leaving the old *sinful* order of things and will find ourselves in a renewed, restored, redeemed creation ... the Bible does not promise us that someday we can *leave* the earth and "go to heaven" instead. Rather, it promises us a whole new creation and includes the earth.

CHRISTOPHER J. H. WRIGHT

Only in heaven—the birthplace of our identity—will we find out who we truly are ... You will not only find what was irretrievably lost, but when you receive it—your new name, your true identity—you will be a thousand times more yourself than the sum total of all those nuances, gestures, and inside subtleties that defined the earthbound "you." On earth you may think you fully blossomed, but heaven will reveal that you barely budded.

JONI EARECKSON TADA

The great street of the city was of gold,
as pure as transparent glass.

REVELATION 21:21

Be honest. Be like any red-blooded, right-thinking Christian with both feet planted firmly on earth ... haven't there been times when word pictures of heaven from the Bible fall flat and boring next to the breathtaking sight and thunderous roar of Niagara Falls? ... You can't ignore streets of gold and rainbow thrones just because they don't thrill you at first glance. They're the images God gave us ... The Bible provides the symbols. But it is faith that makes the hieroglyphics of heaven come alive.

JONI EARECKSON TADA

What Is Heaven Like?

Every beautiful sunset, breathtaking symphony, or exhilarating taste of salt air at the ocean is not merely for your present inspiration. It is a God-sent gift to whet your appetite for your true home in heaven. Earthly pleasures never quite satisfy ... In heaven we will keep getting smarter, wiser, younger, and happier ... one gasp after another, with our joy and amazement ever increasing.

JONI EARECKSON TADA

My best memories give shape to that hopeful future. Your memories—especially if you've lost a loved one, or your health, or your ability to think clearly—should inspire hope in you too. For as wonderful as the world was when all those special remembrances occurred ... these things are only foreshadowings of more delightful, pleasurable experiences to come ... Jesus assures us that our best memories will one day blossom into a more joyous reality than we ever imagined.

JONI EARECKSON TADA

If most of us were honest about how we feel about eternity in heaven, we would have to admit that while heaven sounds like a spectacular place, eternity is a long time. Won't we get bored? Actually, heaven will be a place of complete fulfill-ment and challenging activity and limitless opportunities.

DOUGLAS CONNELLY

You also, like living stones,
are being built into a spiritual house
to be a holy priesthood.

1 PETER 2:5

You and I are living stones, and we are being mined in the quarry of earth, a place of noise, chiseling, and clouds of dust. God is using our sufferings and afflictions to hone and shape us so we might fit perfectly into heaven's landscape, where there is ... no suffering. No tears, pain, sorrow, or death. As polished stones, not only will we fit in heaven, we will fit as glittering jewels in his crown.

JONI EARECKSON TADA

Then I heard what sounded like a great multitude, like the roar of rushing waters and like loud peals of thunder, shouting:

"Hallelujah!
For our Lord God Almighty reigns.
Let us rejoice and be glad
and give him glory!
For the wedding of the Lamb has come,
and his bride has made herself ready.
Fine linen,* bright and clean,
was given her to wear."

REVELATION 19:6–8

*Fine linen stands for the righteous
acts of God's holy people.

By the sea of crystal, saints in glory stand,
Myriads in number, drawn from every land,
Robed in white apparel, washed in Jesus'
    blood,
They now reign in heaven with the Lamb
    of God.

Out of tribulation, death and Satan's hand,
They have been translated at the Lord's
    command.
In their hands they're holding palms of
    victory;
Hark! the jubilant chorus shouts
    triumphantly:

"Unto God Almighty, sitting on the throne,
And the Lamb, victorious, be the praise
    alone,
God has wrought salvation, He did
    wondrous things,
Who shall not extol Thee, holy King of
    Kings?"

WILLIAM KUIPERS, 1932

Then one of the elders asked me, "These in white robes—who are they, and where did they come from?"

I answered, "Sir, you know."

And he said, "These are they who have come out of the great tribulation; they have washed their robes and made them white in the blood of the Lamb.

REVELATION 7:13–14

Heaven will reveal something different [about suffering] … God will personally flip right side up the tangled embroidery of that scarred life to reveal the delicate and beautiful pattern never observed on earth.

JONI EARECKSON TADA

No more charades. No more games.
No more half-truths. Heaven is an honest land.
It is a land where the shadows
are banished by the face of Christ.

MAX LUCADO

I've spent a lot of time yelling at God [after the death of my daughter Maria] ... wanting so badly for the God who I believe in wholeheartedly to yell back all the answers I long to know ... which leaves me yearning for the day when all yelling ceases and every question I had will be answered.

STEVEN CURTIS CHAPMAN

Have you ever said, "You know, I'm going to ask God about that one when I get to heaven." ... You know what I suspect? When we get to heaven and we see Jesus in all of His glory ... there will be but two words we will say concerning the questions of life: "Of course." *Of course!* One glimpse of Him will be all that we shall need for the rest of eternity concerning the mysteries of life.

ZIG ZIGLAR

Heaven will solve our problems, but not, I think, by showing us subtle reconciliations between all our apparently contradictory notions. The notions will all be knocked from under our feet. We shall see that there was never any problem ... that some shattering and disarming simplicity is the real answer.

C. S. Lewis

When Christ calls me Home
I shall go with the gladness
of a boy bounding away from school.

Adoniram Judson,
first Christian missionary to Burma

Soar we now where Christ hath led, Alleluia!
Following our exalted Head, Alleluia!
Made like Him, like Him we rise, Alleluia!
Ours the cross, the grave, the skies, Alleluia!

Charles Wesley, 1739

Will I Know Anyone
in Heaven?

Brothers and sisters, we do not want you to be uninformed about those who sleep in death, so that you do not grieve like the rest of mankind, who have no hope. For we believe that Jesus died and rose again, and so we believe that God will bring with Jesus those who have fallen asleep in him. According to the Lord's word, we tell you that we who are still alive, who are left until the coming of the Lord, will certainly not precede those who have fallen asleep. For the Lord himself will come down from heaven, with a loud command, with the voice of the archangel and with the trumpet call of God, and the dead in Christ will rise first. After that, we who are still alive and are left will be caught up together with them in the clouds to meet the Lord in the air. And so we will be with the Lord forever.

1 THESSALONIANS 4:13–17

Joy pulsated through me as I looked around, and at that moment I became aware of a large crowd of people. They stood in front of a brilliant, ornate gate. As the crowd rushed toward me, I [saw] people I had known ... I felt overwhelmed by the number of people who had come to welcome me to heaven ... and I had never imagined anyone being as happy as they all were. Their faces radiated a serenity I had never seen on earth.

DON PIPER

Will we know [our loved ones] in that land of light, liberty and fullness of joy? By all means! For if Moses and Elijah were recognized on the mount of transfiguration — if Stephen knew his Lord as they were stoning him ... then there is no doubt that we will know one another in that land. We will not lose our identity in heaven and will have the same peculiarities and specific make-up in our entire moral being.

E. M. BOUNDS, 1835 – 1913

Mrs. Glossbrenner was unresponsive for the last few hours of her life. She never spoke a word. But moments before her death, she opened her eyes and stated in a clear voice, "My name is Ida Glossbrenner, but my friends call me Polly." Meaningless words of hallucination? Perhaps. Or, perhaps more. Perhaps Ida was ... at the doors of heaven ... Her soul in the presence of God. And maybe she was getting acquainted.

MAX LUCADO

Those who are victorious will inherit all this [heaven], and I will be their God and they will be my children.

REVELATION 21:7

Heaven is the house where God dwells with his family.

JONATHAN EDWARDS, 1703–1758

How glorious it will be for grandchildren and grandparents — and great-grandchildren and great-grandparents who never knew each other before — to enjoy youth together in the cities, fields, hillsides, and waters of the New Earth. To walk together, discover together, be amazed together — and praise Jesus together.

RANDY ALCORN

I began to think about heaven in a different way. Not just a place with jeweled gates, shining rivers, and streets of gold, but a realm of joy and fellowship ... a place I would one day walk and talk with my grandfather who had meant so much to me, and with the daughter I had never met.

TODD BURPO

Jesus said the institution of marriage would end ... But he never hinted that deep relationships between married people would end ... There's every reason to believe we'll pick right up in Heaven with relationships from Earth ... The notion that relationships with family and friends will be lost in Heaven, though common, is unbiblical ... It completely contradicts Paul's intense anticipation of being with the Thessalonians and his encouraging them to look forward to rejoining their loved ones in Heaven.

RANDY ALCORN

When I get to heaven, I shall see three wonders there. The first wonder will be to see people there I did not expect to see; the second wonder will be to miss many persons whom I did expect to see; and the third and greatest wonder of all will be to find myself there.

JOHN NEWTON, 1725–1807

There is mercy enough in God to admit an innumerable multitude into heaven. There is mercy enough for all, and there is merit enough in Christ to purchase heavenly happiness for millions of millions ... And there is a sufficiency in the fountain of heaven's happiness to supply and fill and satisfy all.

JONATHAN EDWARDS, 1703–1758

*The LORD has established
his throne in heaven,
and his kingdom rules over all.*

PSALM 103:19

Is Heaven Real?

Consider what a joy it will be in heaven, to meet
those there whom you have been the means to
bring thither; to see their faces, and join with
them forever in the praises of God, whom you
were the happy instruments of bringing to the
knowledge and obedience of Jesus Christ!

RICHARD BAXTER, 1615–1691

In Heaven, will we spend time
with people whose lives are recorded
in Scripture and church history?
No doubt.

RANDY ALCORN

*I say to you that many will come from
the east and the west, and will take their
places at the feast with Abraham, Isaac
and Jacob in the kingdom of heaven.*

MATTHEW 8:11

How Do I Get to Heaven?

For God so loved the world that he gave his one and only Son, that whoever believes in him shall not perish but have eternal life.

JOHN 3:16

You are made for a person
and a place.
Jesus is the person.
Heaven is the place.
They are a package—
you cannot get to Heaven
without Jesus.

RANDY ALCORN

"Then the King will say to those on his right, 'Come, you who are blessed by my Father; take your inheritance, the kingdom prepared for you since the creation of the world.'"

MATTHEW 25:34

I frequently hear persons in old age say how they would live, if they were to live their lives over again: Resolved, that I will live just so as I can think I shall wish I had done, supposing I live to old age ... Resolved, to endeavor to my utmost to act as I can think I should do, if I had already seen the happiness of heaven, and hell's torments.

JONATHAN EDWARDS, July 8, 1723

For God did not appoint us to suffer wrath but to receive salvation through our Lord Jesus Christ. He died for us so that ... we may live together with him.

1 THESSALONIANS 5:9–10

Have you said yes to Christ's invitation to join him at the wedding feast and spend eternity with him in his house? If so, you have reason to rejoice — Heaven's gates will be open to you. If you have been putting off your response ... or if you presume that you can enter Heaven without responding to Christ's invitation, one day you will deeply regret it.

RANDY ALCORN

Jesus said to [Martha], "I am the resurrection and the life. The one who believes in me will live, even though they die; and whoever lives by believing in me will never die."

JOHN 11:25–26

If anyone out there is unsure of [how to get to heaven], then for the love of God get out your Bible and study for your finals! To save you time — since you may die while reaching for your Bible — I will quote God's scandalously simple answer to the most important question in the world, how to get to heaven: "Believe in the Lord Jesus, and you will be saved" (Acts 16:31).

PETER KREEFT

"Enter through the narrow gate. For wide is the gate and broad is the road that leads to destruction, and many enter through it. But small is the gate and narrow the road that leads to life, and only a few find it ... Not everyone who says to me, 'Lord, Lord,' will enter the kingdom of heaven, but only the one who does the will of my Father who is in heaven."

MATTHEW 7:13 – 14,21

How worthy is heaven that your life should be wholly spent as a journey towards it. — To what better purpose can you spend your life ... What better end can you propose to your journey, than to obtain heaven? You are placed in this world, with a choice given you ... and one way leads to heaven. Now, can you direct your course better than this way?... How can you better employ your strength, use your means, and spend your days, than in travelling the road that leads to the everlasting enjoyment of God; to his glorious presence; to the new Jerusalem; to the heavenly mount Zion; where all your desires will be filled, and no danger of ever losing your happiness?

JONATHAN EDWARDS, 1703 – 1758

But the day of the Lord will come like a thief. The heavens will disappear with a roar; the elements will be destroyed by fire, and the earth and everything done in it will be laid bare. Since everything will be destroyed in this way, what kind of people ought you to be? You ought to live holy and godly lives as you look forward to the day of God and speed its coming.

2 PETER 3:10–12

How Do I Get to Heaven?

Come to the better land,
Pilgrim, make haste;
Earth is a foreign strand,
Wilderness waste.
Here are the harps of gold,
Here are the joys untold,
Crowns for the young and old;
Come, pilgrim, come.

Jesus, we come to Thee,
O take us in!
Set Thou our spirits free,
Cleanse us from sin.
Then, in yon land of light,
Clothed in our robes of white,
Resting not day nor night,
Thee will we sing.

HENRY BURTON, 1840-1930

*Rejoice that your names
are written in heaven.*

LUKE 10:20

Sing the wondrous love of Jesus,
Sing His mercy and His grace.
In the mansions bright and blessed
He'll prepare for us a place.

When we all get to Heaven,
What a day of rejoicing that will be!
When we all see Jesus,
We'll sing and shout the victory!

Let us then be true and faithful,
Trusting, serving every day;
Just one glimpse of Him in glory
Will the toils of life repay.

Onward to the prize before us!
Soon His beauty we'll behold;
Soon the pearly gates will open;
We shall tread the streets of gold.

ELIZA HEWITT, 1898

Set your minds on things above, not on earthly things. For you died, and your life is now hidden with Christ in God. When Christ, who is your life, appears, then you also will appear with him in glory.

COLOSSIANS 3:2–4

There is nothing but heaven
worth setting your hearts upon ...
A heart, therefore, set upon heaven,
is a heart set upon God.

RICHARD BAXTER, 1615–1691

"Do not store up for yourselves treasures on earth, where moths and vermin destroy, and where thieves break in and steal. But store up for yourselves treasures in heaven, where moths and vermin do not destroy, and where thieves do not break in and steal. For where your treasure is, there your heart will be also."

MATTHEW 6:19–21

Why should my heart be fixed
where my home is not?
Heaven is my home;
God in Christ is all my happiness:
and where my treasure is,
there my heart should be.

MARGARET CHARLTON BAXTER, 1631–1681

God has given us eternal life, and this life is in his Son. Whoever has the Son has life; whoever does not have the Son of God does not have life. I write these things to you who believe in the name of the Son of God so that you may know that you have eternal life.

1 JOHN 5:11–13

You have no right to heaven in yourself: your right lies in Christ. If you are pardoned, it is through his blood; if you are justified, it is through his righteousness ... and if you are perfected at the last, it will be because you are complete in him. Thus Jesus is magnified ... and even heaven itself the brighter, because it is Jesus our Beloved "in whom" we have obtained all.

CHARLES SPURGEON, 1834–1893

"I tell you ... there will be more rejoicing in heaven over one sinner who repents than over ninety-nine righteous persons who do not need to repent."

LUKE 15:7

For to me, to live is Christ and to die is gain.

PHILIPPIANS 1:21

Finally . . .

In mansions of glory and endless
  delight,
I'll ever adore Thee in heaven
  so bright;
I'll sing with the glittering crown
  on my brow;
If ever I loved Thee, my Jesus,
  'tis now.

WILLIAM R. FEATHERSTON, 1846–1873,
    written when he was only 16

*I will dwell
in the house of the LORD
forever.*

PSALM 23:6

Acknowledgments

Is Heaven Real?

Page 11: Michael Faraday, users.belgacom.net/gc674645/
prose/heavquot.htm.

Page 12: Randy Alcorn, *Heaven*, (Carol Stream, Ill.:
Tyndale, 2004), 443.

Page 12: Bernard of Morlaix, "Jerusalem the Golden,"
www.cyberhymnal.org, 1146.

Page 13: Lee Strobel, *God's Outrageous Claims*, (Grand
Rapids, Mich.: Zondervan, 2005), 220.

Page 14: Calvin Miller, *The Divine Symphony*, (Grand
Rapids, Mich.: Bethany, 2000), 139.

Page 15: Peter Kreeft, www.peterkreeft.com/topics/
heaven.htm.

Page 16: Jerry Sittser, *A Grace Disguised*, (Grand Rapids,
Mich.: Zondervan, 2004), 193.

Page 16: Peter Kreeft, www.peterkreeft.com/topics/
heaven.htm.

Page 17: Dave Dravecky, "The Encourager," Spring 1996;
taken from *Glimpses of Heaven*, by Dave and Jan
Dravecky (Grand Rapids, Mich.: Zondervan, 1996), 12.

Page 17: Charles Wesley, "Love Divine, All Loves
Excelling," www.cyberhymnal.com.

Page 18: Joni Eareckson Tada, *Heaven ... Your Real Home*,
Devotional Edition, (Grand Rapids, Mich.: Zondervan,
1996), 70.

Page 19: Strobel, *God's Outrageous Claims*, 203.

Page 21: Charles Spurgeon, *Morning and Evening*, September 7, www.ccel.org.

Page 22: Sanford F. Bennett, "In the Sweet By and By," www.cyberhymnal.org.

Page 23: Mary Beth Chapman, *Choosing to See*, (Grand Rapids, Mich.: Revell, 2010), 145.

Page 25: Dwight L. Moody, www.jesus-is-savior.com.

Page 26: Dwight L. Moody, www.christian-quotes.com.

Page 27: Richard Baxter, *Saints' Everlasting Rest*, www.ccel.org/ccel/baxter/saints_rest.iii.III.html.

Page 28: C. S. Lewis, *Mere Christianity*, (San Francisco: HarperOne, 2001), 136.

Page 29: A. W. Tozer, *Glimpses of Heaven*, (Grand Rapids, Mich.: Zondervan, 1996), 134.

Page 30: C. S. Lewis, *The Problem of Pain*, (New York: Macmillan, 1962), 148.

Page 31: John Donne, users.belgacom.net/gc674645/prose/heavquot.htm.

What Is Heaven Like?

Page 36: Max Lucado, *The Applause of Heaven*, (Carol Stream, Ill: Tyndale, 1995), 186.

Page 36: Baxter, *The Saints' Everlasting Rest*, www.ccel.org.

Page 37: Charles Spurgeon, *Morning and Evening*, April 25, www.ccel.org.

Page 37: Todd Burpo, *Heaven Is Real*, (Nashville: Thomas Nelson, 2010), 103.

Acknowledgments

Page 38: Francis M. Knollis, "There Is No Night in Heaven," www.cyberhymnal.org.

Page 38: Charles Spurgeon, *Morning and Evening*, January 29, www.ccel.org.

Page 39: Fanny Crosby, "Saved by Graced," www.cyberhymnal.org.

Page 40: Helen Keller, users.belgacom.net/gc674645/prose/heavquot.htm.

Page 40: Jonathan Edwards, www.goodreads.com.

Page 41: Tada, *Heaven ... Your Real Home*, 124.

Page 41: Joni Eareckson Tada, quoted in Philip Yancy, *Where Is God When It Hurts*, (Grand Rapids, Mich.: Zondervan, 1990), 136.

Page 42: Alcorn, *Heaven*, 351.

Page 42: Tada, *Heaven ... Your Real Home*, 49.

Page 43: Frederick Buechner, quoted in *A Little Bit of Heaven*, (Tulsa, Okla.: Honor Books, 1995), 118.

Page 43: Margaret Charlton Baxter, www.thequotablechristian.com.

Page 44: Don Piper, *90 Minutes in Heaven*, (Grand Rapids, Mich.: Revell, 2004), 30.

Page 44: Tada, *Heaven ... Your Real Home*, 16.

Page 45: Frederick M. Lehman, "There's No Disappointment in Heaven," www.cyberhymal.org.

Page 46: Alcorn, *Heaven*, 442.

Page 47: Zig Ziglar, *Confessions of a Grieving Christian*, (Nashville: Broadman & Holman, 2004), 95.

Page 47: Peter Kreeft, *Heaven: The Heart's Deepest Longing*, (San Francisco: Harper and Row, 1980), 125.

Page 48: Welsh hymn, www.gutenberg.org.

Page 49: L. B. Cowman, *Streams in the Desert: 366 Daily Devotional Reading*, ed. James Reimann (Grand Rapids, Mich.: Zondervan, 1997), 487–88.

Page 50: D. L. Moody, quoted in *A Home Beyond: or Views of Heaven*, Samuel Fallows, ed. (Chicago: The National Library Association, 1889), 344.

Page 50: Tada, *Heaven ... Your Real Home*, 59.

Page 51: Martin Luther, www.brainyquote.com.

Page 51: Piper, *90 Minutes in Heaven*, 25.

Page 53: Christopher J. H. Wright, *The God I Don't Understand*, (Grand Rapids, Mich.: Zondervan, 2008), 195.

Page 53: Tada, *Heaven ... Your Real Home*, 94.

Page 54: Tada, *Heaven ... Your Real Home*, 12–13.

Page 55: Joni Eareckson Tada, *Pearls of Great Price*, (Grand Rapids: Zondervan, 2006), May 23.

Page 55: Tada, *Pearls of Great Price*, October 22.

Page 56: Douglas Connelly, *The Promise of Heaven: Discovering Our Eternal Home*, (Downers Grove, Ill.: InterVarsity, 2000), 125.

Page 57: Tada, *Pearls of Great Price*, December 8.

Page 59: William Kuipers, "By the Sea of Crystal," www. cyberhymnal.org.

Page 60: Tada, *Pearls of Great Price*, July 7.

Page 60: Max Lucado, *When Christ Comes*, (Dallas, Texas: Word, 1999), 136.

Page 61: Steven Curtis Chapman, quoted in Mary Beth Chapman, *Choosing to See*, (Grand Rapids, Mich.: Revell, 2010), 263.

Page 61: Ziglar, *Confessions of a Grieving Christian*, 252.

Page 62: C. S. Lewis, *A Grief Observed*, (San Francisco: HarperSanFrancisco, 1961), 71.

Page 62: Adoniram Judson, users.belgacom.net/gc674645/prose/heavquot.htm.

Page 62: Charles Wesley, "Christ the Lord Is Risen Today," www.cyberhymnal.org.

Will I Know Anyone in Heaven?

Page 66: Piper, *90 Minutes in Heaven*, 21, 24.

Page 66: E. M. Bounds, *Catching a Glimpse of Heaven*, (Pittsburgh, Penn.: Whitaker House, 1985), 138–39.

Page 67: Lucado, *When Christ Comes*, 38.

Page 67: Jonathan Edwards, "Sinners in the Hands of an Angry God," www.ccel.org.

Page 68: Alcorn, *Heaven*, 351.

Page 68: Burpo, *Heaven Is Real*, 103.

Page 69: Alcorn, *Heaven*, 337.

Page 70: John Newton, www.family-times.net.

Page 70: Jonathan Edwards, "Many Mansions" from *Select Sermons*, www.ccel.org/ccel/edwards/sermons.

Page 72: Baxter, *Saints' Everlasting Rest*, www.ccel.org.

Page 72: Alcorn, *Heaven*, 345.

How Do I Get to Heaven?

Page 75: Alcorn, *Heaven*, 37.

Page 76: Jonathan Edwards, "Many Mansions," July 8, 1723, www.apuritansmind.com.

Page 77: Alcorn, *Heaven*, 32.

Page 78: Kreeft, www.peterkreeft.com/topics/heaven.htm.

Page 79: Jonathan Edwards, *Works of Jonathan Edwards*, volume 2, www.ccel.org.

Page 81: Henry Burton, "Come, for the Feast Is Spread," *Psalter Hymnal* (Grand Rapids, Mich.: Publication Committee of the Christian Reformed Church, 1840–1930), 420.

Page 82: Eliza Hewitt, "When We All Get to Heaven," www.cyberhymnal.org.

Page 83: Baxter, *Saints' Everlasting Rest*, www.ccel.org.

Page 84: Margaret Charlton Baxter, www.thequotablechristian.com.

Page 85: Charles Spurgeon, *Morning and Evening*, January 30, www.ccel.org.

Finally ...

Page 89: William R. Featherston, "My Jesus, I Love Thee," www.cyberhymnal.org.